Ava Loves Rescuing Animals

happy yak

Brimming with creative inspiration, how-to projects, and useful information to enrich your everyday life, quarto.com is a favorite destination for those pursuing their interests and passions.

Jess French has asserted her right to be identified as the author of this work. Duncan Beedie has asserted his right to be identified as the illustrator of this work.

Designer: Mike Henson
Commissioning Editor: Emily Pither
Editor: Victoria Garrard
Creative Director: Malena Stojić
Associate Publisher: Rhiannon Findlay

First published in 2023 by Happy Yak, an imprint of The Quarto Group.
100 Cummings Center, Suite 265D
Beverly, MA 01915, USA.
T (978) 282-9590 F (978) 283-2742
www.quarto.com

A CIP record for this book is available from the Library of Congress.

ISBN 978-0-7112-6773-2
eBook ISBN 978-0-7112-6772-5

Manufactured in Guangdong, China TT122022

9 8 7 6 5 4 3 2 1

STAY SAFE!

Meeting animals is great fun if you follow these guidelines to keep you safe:

- Always treat animals kindly.

- Move slowly and quietly around animals so you do not scare them.

- Always ask for the owner's permission before touching a pet and always follow the owner's advice on how to act around their pet.

- Don't go near any wild animals unless a grown-up says it is ok.

- If you find an animal that needs rescuing, don't touch it or go near it. Instead, ask an adult.

- Never chase wild animals.

- Don't touch anything that comes from an animal such as fur, feathers, shed skin, or poop unless a grown-up says it is safe.

- Always wash your hands with soap and water after touching anything that comes from an animal.

- Don't feed wild animals.

JESS FRENCH

DUNCAN BEEDIE

Ava Loves
Rescuing Animals

Hi, I'm Mini, Ava's pet mouse. I like to join her on her animal adventures!

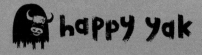

happy yak

HELLO, I'M AVA, I LOVE ANIMALS. I live with my grandparents. They run an animal rescue center. It's amazing!

There are always lots of fluffy and feathered friends here, sometimes in very unexpected places!

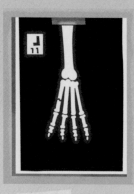

Is it morning?

Hello Mini, were you snoozing again?

Animals come to the rescue center for all sorts of reasons. We look after them until they are well enough to go back into the wild, or to a new home.

This is Grandad. He's a vet. When animals come in feeling poorly, he helps them.

And this is Grandma. She's preparing for a new animal arrival. I wonder what it will be?

Whatever it is, we will take great care of it.

5

We're preparing a comfy space for our new resident.

Water bottle

Big pen

Shelter to hide in

Food bowl

Where's the hot tub?

Snuggly straw

Newspaper to soak up any droppings

Grandma says our new arrival loves to gobble up hay, but we've run out so I will walk to the pet shop.

Can you guess what animal it might be?

Morning **kittens!** These cuties are waiting for their new forever homes. We give them plenty of cuddles while they wait.

Cats come here for all sorts of reasons. Sometimes they have no home, or they have had to leave their owners.

This is Bambi. She's a baby **deer**, which is a **fawn**. We are looking after her until she's big enough to go outside in the paddock with the adults.

What a cozy stable. I wonder if there's time for a nap?

Mother animals often leave their babies for a short time to go and get food. Wildlife rescuers watch the babies for a long time before deciding if they need help. If you think an animal is in trouble, tell a grown-up.

7

I love all animals, from the ones we rescue at the center, to the ones that live far away such as elephants and tigers.

WILD ANIMALS

All animals were wild once. Wild animals live in their natural habitats and include everything from a squirrel to a killer whale! Humans do not give these animals food, water, or shelter.

Squirrel

Bee

Tiger

Elephant

Bear

Kangaroo

Chimpanzee

Killer whale

Eagle

Which wild animals have you seen in your local area?

PETS

Cats and **dogs** are the most popular pets but people keep other animals too. Pets live with us in our homes and rely on us for everything—food, drink, exercise, shelter, and love!

Guinea pig

Mouse

Hamster

Gerbil

Ferret

Degu

Chinchilla

Budgie

Mini is a great pet—
she makes me laugh,
is cuddly, and loves
to come with me on
adventures!

You're
a great
owner too!

Having a pet is a big responsibility so you need to make sure the pet you choose suits your home and your family's lifestyle. To your pet, you are its everything.

A walk can quickly turn into an adventure so I make sure I'm prepared. Here's what I pack:

Always take a grown-up with you on nature walks.

Sun hat

Water

Boots

Coat

Camera

Map

ID guides

Any space for me?

Flashlight

Sunscreen

Spare socks

Watch

Snacks

Whistle

And most importantly, my camera, to record everything I find.

Magnifying glass

I'll just check the pond before we leave. Ooh, the **frogs** have laid some more frogspawn, which will hatch into tadpoles.

CLICK!

Tadpoles will grow into frogs. Eventually they will lose their tails, grow four strong legs, and hop away to make a home on the land.

The life cycle of a frog

2 The eggs hatch into tadpoles. They have gills which allow them to breathe underwater.

1 A frog lays a clump of jelly-like eggs called frogspawn.

3 After a few weeks, the tadpoles start to grow legs.

As the tadpoles grow, their bodies totally change shape. This is called metamorphosis.

5 The froglet leaves the water and becomes a frog.

4 The tadpole loses its tail and becomes a froglet.

Amphibians

Frogs are part of a group called amphibians.
Adult amphibians can spend time both in and out of the water.

Toads often have bumpy skin and move by crawling.

Newts are salamanders that spend a lot of time in water.

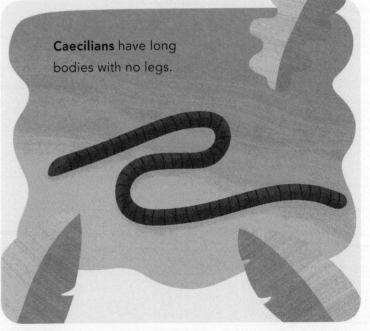

Salamanders look a lot like lizards but have smooth, wet skin instead of scales.

Caecilians have long bodies with no legs.

It's a beautiful sunny day.
Look, there's a snake!

I won't get too close, but look at its scaly skin and forked tongue.

Never approach a **snake** as some have a dangerous bite.

"Hi Ava. Check out my new bike!"

"Watch out Pedro— there's a **lizard**!"

"Off you go little friend.
Find somewhere safe to rest."

EEK!
I think I'll stay
up here!

CLICK!

Some lizards and snakes can
flick out their tongues to taste
the air. This helps them to find
food and avoid danger.

REPTILES

Reptiles have bodies that are protected by scales and they shed their skin as they grow. They use the heat of the sun to warm themselves up. Most of them lay eggs.

Snakes have long, thin bodies and no legs. They grab their food with their mouths and swallow it whole.

burp!

Lizards usually have long tails and four legs. They live all over the world in lots of different environments.

Turtles have webbed feet or flippers.

Crocodiles have thick scales and strong jaws. They are expert hunters, often attacking and eating animals much larger than themselves.

Tortoises have hard shells and stumpy, rounded legs. They spend most of their time on dry land.

Alligators have broad snouts and are usually found in fresh water.

"Snakes are my favorite reptile. I sometimes see them sunbathing!"

Most reptiles can't make their own body heat and rely on the sun's rays to warm them up.

"I sometimes find their old skins."

Every now and again, reptiles shed their old skin. A new one grows underneath!

"I better go. We need to buy some hay for our latest animal rescue."

"That's exciting. I'm off to the recycling center."

Great! Time for a snooze.

It's important to stick to the path when you're walking through the countryside, so you don't disturb any wildlife.

Birds may be sheltering under hedgerows.

Lizards may be nesting in piles of twigs.

Butterflies may be feeding on nectar.

It is important to follow the Countryside Code to keep everyone safe.

Always ask for a grown-up's advice before entering a field, even if the signs say you are allowed.

The track we need to follow is just over this stile.

You can squeeze through that gap, Mini.

Limbo!

Gaps like this allow mice and other small mammals to pass through.

Stiles allow people to pass, but keep large animals in.

Mammals

Mammals can make their own heat, so they don't need to rely on the sun to keep them warm. This means they can live in cold places like the Arctic.

They are covered in hair or fur.

They produce milk for their babies to drink.

They come in all shapes and sizes.

21

ANIMAL RECORD BREAKERS

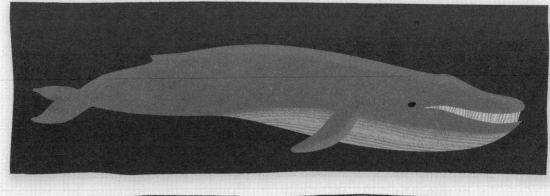

The biggest animal is the **blue whale**—it is longer than two school buses!

The fastest land animal is the **cheetah**. When it is running, its feet spend more time in the air than on the ground!

The smallest mammal is the **bumblebee bat**. It is around the same size as a bumblebee.

The tallest animal is the **giraffe**. An adult human doesn't even reach its shoulder!

The heaviest land animal is the **African elephant** —it's about three times heavier than a rhino!

The smallest reptile is a **nano chameleon**—it's the size of a seed.

The longest insect is a **giant stick insect**. It's about as long as a human arm!

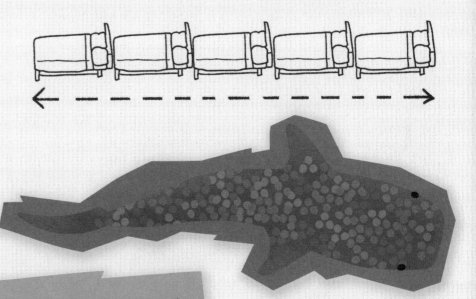

The biggest fish is the **whale shark**—it's as long as five double beds!

We're heading through the farm now, there are lots of animals to meet. Moo! Hello cows!

Cows have strong flexible tongues for pulling up grass.

Baa! Hello sheep! I love how the **lambs** waggle their tails.

Counting these sheep is making me sleepy!

Baby **sheep** drink milk from their mothers to help them grow big and strong.

Oink! Hello pigs! Looks like you've been wallowing in the mud. I bet that keeps you nice and cool.

Rolling in mud protects a **pig's** delicate skin from the sun.

Cluck, cluck! Watch out chickens! Are you enjoying your dust bath?

Chickens bathe themselves in dust to get rid of oil and tiny bugs, and to keep their feathers clean.

These farm animals are all known as livestock. This means they produce something that people use.

Cows are kept to make milk, meat, and leather.

Pigs are kept to make meat and leather.

Chickens are kept to make meat and eggs.

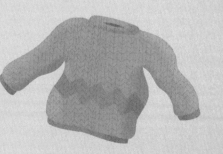

Sheep are kept to make meat, milk, and wool.

There are some dried prints here. I think they might be horse hoof prints but I'll check in my book...

Wow, this animal has BIG feet!

CLICK!

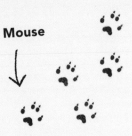

Find the Footprints

Chicken

Deer

Mouse

Fox

Horse

Hello horses! You look like you are enjoying the sunshine.

Baby horses are called **foals**. They can walk within a few hours of being born.

People dress **horses** in saddles and bridles so they can ride them.

This one looks a bit like a horse, but its ears are much bigger. It must be a donkey!

HEE-HAW!

Donkeys and horses are closely related and often live together.

HEE-HAW to you!

"Hi Ava. This is Baxter."

Dogs are mammals. They have lived with people for thousands of years.

Dogs with Jobs

Many dogs are kept as pets, but lots of dogs have important jobs too!

Guide dogs help people that cannot see very well to find their way.

Sniffer dogs find things that are hidden.

Herding dogs help to round up cows and sheep.

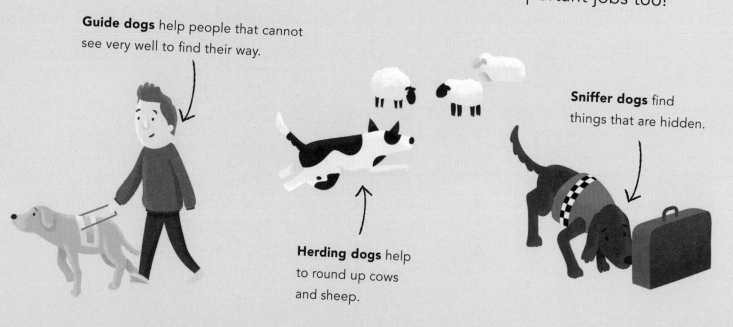

28

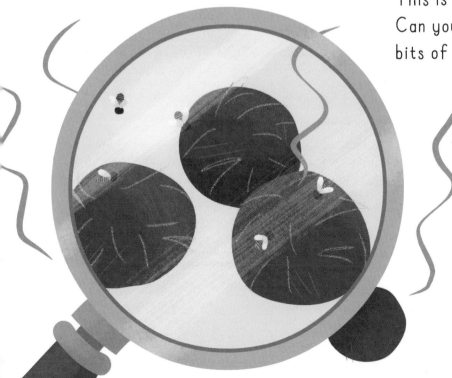

"We take Baxter on two walks every day. He loves to sniff around."

It is important to keep dogs on a leash in places where they could disturb wildlife.

What have you found, Baxter? Ooh look at all those flies. Let's take a closer look.

This is horse poop! Can you see little bits of grass?

It sounds a bit yucky, but baby **dung flies** love to munch on dung. If we didn't have recyclers like flies to get rid of all the animal poop, it would be everywhere!

Flies are insects. Insects are animals too. In fact they make up 90 percent of all types of animals on the planet!

Poop is fascinating! Many animals can be identified by their poop, which is really helpful if you are tracking them!

An animal's poop can also tell us what they have been eating or if they are sick.

Some poops are small.

Like chocolate chips.

Rabbit poop

WHOA! A mouse could get lost in that!

Some poops are big.

We can often tell what group an animal belongs to by the look of its poop. Look out for feathers, bones, twigs, or grass in the poop.

Elephant poop

ANIMAL GROUPS

1 Carnivores are animals that only eat other animals.

Dolphins work together to catch fish.

Frogs gobble up insects and worms.

Lions hunt zebras and antelopes on the savannas of Africa.

Alligators have powerful jaws to grab their prey.

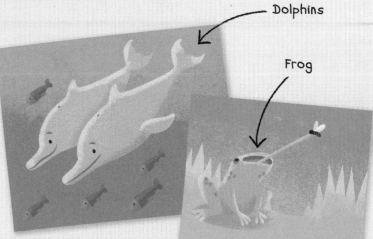

Dolphins

Frog

Badger

Capuchin monkey

2 Omnivores eat a mix of meat and plants.

Badgers eat bulbs, berries, insects, and small mammals.

Capuchin monkeys eat fruits, leaves, eggs, and insects.

Grizzly bears eat fruit, berries, nuts, fish, and meat.

Pet dogs eat meat, vegetables, and grains.

3 Herbivores only eat plants.

Rhinos eat branches, grasses, and leaves.

Koalas eat eucalyptus leaves.

Iguanas eat flowers, fruit, and leaves.

Wildebeest graze on grasses.

Rhino

Koala

"Billy, you scared me!
I didn't see you there."

"I've been trying to spot some birds
from my hide. Would you like to see?"

When people or animals look like their surroundings, we say they are camouflaged.

A hide is a shelter that is used to watch wildlife close up.

Look over there by the sea. Can you see the birds, catching food with their long beaks?

Oh yes. They look like they are on stilts!

Better than a knife and fork.

32

"Oh no! That naughty cat has frightened the birds away."

"I'm going to head down to the beach on my way to the pet shop. I want to see what animals are there today. Thank you for showing me your hide. I hope the birds come back soon!"

WHOOOSH

Ecosystems

In the wild, lots of different animals and plants can live together in one place. We call this shared environment an **ecosystem**.

FOOD CHAINS

Within the ecosystem, different plants and animals have different roles depending on the food they eat:

- Food chains often start with plants. These plants are called producers.

- Some animals are hunted and eaten by other animals. The animals that are hunted are called prey.

- Some animals catch other animals and eat them as food. These are called predators.

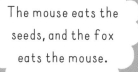

The mouse eats the seeds, and the fox eats the mouse.

Seeds (producer)

Mouse (prey)

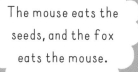

Fox (predator)

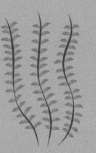

Underwater plants (producer)

Fish (prey)

Bear (predator)

34

FOOD WEBS

In the wild, it's a bit more complicated. Producers and prey are eaten by lots of different animals, and some of those animals eat one another too! We show this by drawing a food web.

Killer Whale (Orca)

Blue whale

Leopard seal

Gull

Penguin

Fish

Elephant seal

Zooplankton

Seaweed

Phytoplankton

Squid

Crab

I love seeing ocean animals at the beach.

What's that scuttling across the beach?
It has ten legs and walks sideways...

It's a **crab**!

There's something else down
there too...it's a **turtle**.

Oh no, there's a bit of plastic
wrapped around its neck.

"Don't worry turtle, we will
soon set you free."

Plastic is really dangerous for sea creatures.
Not only can they eat it, thinking it is food,
but they can get tangled up in it too.

Grandma is trained in animal rescue
and always carries an emergency box
in case we come across any injured
animals. It contains useful things like
bandages, scissors, and gloves.

Recycling bin

What?
No food?

I wasn't expecting to see a turtle today!
We will put this plastic in the recycling bin.
Picking up litter is a great way to protect
animals from human trash.

HABITATS AND HOMES

The environment that an animal lives in is called a habitat.

Temperate forests change with the seasons. **Squirrels** can be found scurrying through trees in temperate forests.

Coastal habitats are on the border between land and sea. Crabs can be found in rock pools at the coast.

Deserts are often very hot and dry. Animals that live in the desert, such as **meerkats**, must be able to survive without much water.

The open ocean is the world's biggest habitat. Huge shoals of fish can be found in the open ocean.

Polar habitats are icy and cold. **Polar bears** live on sea ice.

Only very specialized animals can live in mountain habitats. **Mountain goats** are brilliant at clambering across rocky cliff faces.

Rivers and most lakes are freshwater habitats. **Water voles** make their homes in river banks.

Grasslands are also known as savanna, pampas, prairies, and rangelands. Herds of **zebra** graze on savannas in Africa.

We have made it to the pet shop at last.

Have you found something you would like, Mini?

Bowls

Pet toothbrushes and toothpaste

Collars

Toys

Dog food

Cat food

Any mouse treats?

Brushes

Cozy beds

Leashes

Cat litter

Scratching post

Now we have the hay, we should hurry home to meet our new arrival!

This path along the river leads back to the rescue center.

Something has been gnawing on this tree. I wonder what it could be?

These paw prints and this poop came from an **otter**...

...but otters don't gnaw on trees!

FISH

Fish are animals that live in the water. They have fins instead of legs and their bodies are often covered in scales. They have gills, so they can breathe underwater.

Seahorses swim upright and have long snouts.

Lionfish have venomous spines.

Clownfish live in anemones.

Parrotfish munch on coral.

Tuna shoot through the water like torpedoes.

Sharks are excellent hunters.

Our new arrival is here, and there is more than one! We are putting the finishing touches to their enclosure. That looks cozy.

Our new residents are small and fluffy...

...with long ears,

huge feet,

and cute, fluffy tails!

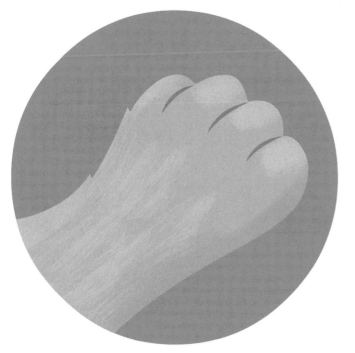

They are **rabbits!**

Their owner had to go into the hospital so we will look after them for her.

45

Aw, it looks like the rabbits are cozy, snuggled up together—they don't like being alone. It's almost time for me to go to sleep too.

Before bed there is just enough time to snuggle up and look at some of the photos I took today.

There might be time to read one of my favorite animal books too!

Oh! What a great day!

It's easy to get to know the animals that live near you. Look out for clues like footprints and poop. Then all you have to do is wait and watch. Good luck!

HOW TO BE A
NATURE HERO
≡ANIMALS≡

Our world is full of extraordinary creatures, from the pets that share our homes to the wild animals that roam on distant shores. The things we do every day impact all of these animals. Follow these guidelines and you can be a real life ANIMAL HERO!

- Become a volunteer dog walker. Your local rehoming center might need volunteers, or you could see if any elderly neighbors need a dog walker.

- Plant a tree. One day it will provide food and shelter for lots of different animals.

- Organize a beach clean up. Picking up litter stops ocean creatures from eating or getting tangled up in plastic.

- Use your voice. Tell your family and friends everything you have learned about endangered animals and how to help them.

To protect all animals and the world they live in, it is also important to:

- Think carefully before buying new things. Try to avoid buying plastic and buy things secondhand whenever you can.

- Treat wild spaces with kindness—pick up litter, stick to the paths, and never trample on plants or fungi.

- Grow green things wherever you can. Pack your windowsill with plants or create a vegetable patch.

Pedro   Billy   Bella